W9-AMN-791

BAD BREATH—AND LOTS OF IT!

"Burping cows must rank as the number-one source of air pollution in the U.S.," states the Environmental Protection Agency. According to the agency, "Ten cows burp enough gas in a year to provide all the space-heating, water-heating, and cooking requirements of a small house."

**ENCYCLOPEDIA BROWN'S
BOOK OF WACKY ANIMALS**

Bantam Skylark Books by Donald J. Sobol
Ask your bookseller for the books you have missed

DONALD J. SOBOL

Encyclopedia Brown's Book of Wacky ANIMALS

Illustrated by Ted Enik

A BANTAM SKYLARK BOOK®
TORONTO • NEW YORK • LONDON • SYDNEY • AUCKLAND

AUTHOR'S NOTE

All the incidents reported in this book are true.

—DONALD J. SOBOL

RL 6, 008–012

ENCYCLOPEDIA BROWN'S BOOK OF WACKY ANIMALS
A Bantam Book / published by arrangement with the author

PRINTING HISTORY
William Morrow edition published April 1985
Bantam Skylark edition / September 1985

ISBN 0-553-15346-3

Published simultaneously in the United States and Canada

PRINTED IN THE UNITED STATES OF AMERICA

CW   0 9 8 7 6 5 4 3 2 1

For Tony and Pauli Reinert

Contents

Introduction

During the summer Encyclopedia Brown ran a detective agency in the family garage. Most of his customers were children of the neighborhood. But now and then he was called upon to solve a mystery for a grown-up.

Early one morning in August, Mrs. Randall telephoned the 10-year-old sleuth. She wanted to hire him. Could he come at once?

It was before business hours, but Encyclopedia said he'd be right over.

He scribbled a note to Sally Kimball, his junior partner, telling her where he was going. Then he hopped on his bike.

After a few minutes of fast pedaling, Encyclopedia reached Mrs. Randall's house on Foxfire Lane. She was waiting for him by the front steps.

"Have a look at this mess," she said, leading him to her car and then to her back porch and clothesline.

All three were covered with yellow splotches.

"Is that glop ever hard to remove!" Mrs. Randall exclaimed. "At first I thought some children were playing a prank with mustard or iodine. Now I don't know."

Encyclopedia examined the splotches. He glanced up and down the block.

"Are there any melaleuca trees in blossom around here?" he asked.

The question took Mrs. Randall by surprise. "Why, yes," she answered. "It so happens there are. Lots of them."

"The trees are half the problem," Encyclopedia said. He explained. Mrs. Randall listened, frowning. When Encyclopedia was done, she paid him his fee, twenty-five cents, and walked unhappily into the house.

Back at the detective agency, Encyclopedia found Sally seated at the desk, ready for business.

"How'd it go?" she inquired.

"Fine," Encyclopedia said. "It was a honey of a case."

He described the yellow splotches. "What do you think caused them?" he asked.

Sally shrugged. "What?"

"Bees dripping wax on the way to the hive," Encyclopedia answered. "Around this time of year, bees gather a mixture of nectar and pollen from blossoming melaleuca trees and carry it as wax in little pockets on their legs. When the bees have to turn a corner in flight, they often spill some of it."

2

"Mrs. Randall must have been pleased that you solved the mystery so quickly," Sally said.

"Nope," Encyclopedia replied. "Beeswax flights usually last about a month. That means Mrs. Randall's neighborhood is in for three more sticky weeks. She wasn't too happy."

Sally was smiling. "I'm sorry for Mrs. Randall," she said. "Still, it was a rather funny case, wasn't it? You know something? You ought to start a collection of funny true stories about insects and all sorts of animals."

Encyclopedia had already shown Sally his scrapbooks filled with true stories of wacky crimes, wacky sports, and wacky spies. He stepped to the shelves at the rear of the detective agency. From the top shelf he took down a large green scrapbook.

"Oh, don't tell me you've already started a scrapbook of wacky animal stories!" Sally cried.

Encyclopedia grinned. He opened the green scrapbook on the desk. "Care to have a look?"

"Would I!" Sally said, and she began to read. . . .

I.

Thereby Hangs a Tail

Beauty is in the eyes of the beholder. All together now, who was Beauty?

No, not Sleeping Beauty.

The answer is Beauty the chimpanzee, who rocked the world of modern art in 1961.

Beauty's career began as a publicity stunt for the yearly Arts Festival at the Cincinnati Zoo. A zoo official made a daring suggestion, Why not teach a chimp to paint? Then the animals would have one of their own in the art show.

Teach a chimp to paint . . . seriously?

Why not?

The most gifted of the chimps turned out to be a 3-year-old female named Beauty. Her finger-painted watercolors were considered good enough, as modern

art goes, to be put on exhibition. They became the hit of the Arts Festival. Overnight, the price of her pictures soared from nothing to $25 unframed, $50 framed.

Word of the ape artist reached New York City, where paintings no one can understand always go over big. Within six months Beauty's paintings reached the heights. Her one-chimp show was booked at the fashionable Bianchi Gallery in Manhattan. Critics, journalists, and TV crews flocked to the champagne opening.

Beauty's five-color paintings on cardboard were priced from $35 to $95. They sold so quickly that a hurried call went out to the zoo for more.

At the age of 3, Beauty had become more famous than Leonardo da Vinci (at the age of 3). Yet she missed all the fuss and fanfare. Throughout her show's two-week run, she remained at home and never took a bow. A zoo spokesman explained that she might catch pneumonia if she were brought to New York City. (Chimps are prone to pneumonia.)

Unaware of her fame, Beauty painted furiously for a few minutes daily—she had a short attention span. The rest of the day she had a swinging good time with her nonpainting partner, Bean, and their buddies, a husky dog, a pony, and a baby elephant.

After her New York show closed, Beauty continued painting for a brief time only. She left the zoo in 1965 for a breeding farm in California. Her death passed unnoticed. She had outlived her days as New York City's top banana.

All choked up. A man rushed into a government building in Nairobi, Kenya, in 1983, and broke a glass display case containing a stuffed lion. The offender began to choke the animal violently.

After his arrest, the man told the police that his brother had been slain by a lion. He had vowed to avenge his death by killing one of the beasts with his bare hands.

Say it with music. A man climbed a 10-foot concrete wall at the Honolulu Zoo in 1982, stripped down to his underwear, and played a harmonica for an elephant.

Empress, a 51-year-old female Indian elephant, knew what she liked in music, and an off-key harmonica wasn't it. Roused to a mild temper, she cornered the man. After he was rescued, police charged him with cruelty to animals.

Tusk, tusk.

Mind your manners. It happened on a farm near Zacata, Virginia, in 1933. Seems the farmer was feeding his stallion when a hog came up to the trough. Bold as you please, the hog poked its snout into the corn.

Angered, the horse lifted the 90-pound hog by a leg, carried it 30 feet to the well, and dropped it in. The farmer had to buy a new rope to rescue the hog, which never again tried to steal the horse's feed.

That dwedful rabbit. Near Louisville, Kentucky, in 1947, a rabbit worked its paw out of a hunter's game bag, accidentally tapped the trigger of his gun, and shot him in the foot. *Moral:* Beware the gun with a hare trigger.

Falling in love again. A moose in Nova Scotia fell head-over-antlers in love with a foghorn.

In mid-October, 1982, the moose swam across a mile of ocean from Arichat to Green Island. The haunting tones of the island's foghorn, amazingly similar to the moose mating call, beckoned with the promise of sweet romance.

Scientists took pity on the misguided moose. They planned to drug him and then airlift him off the tree-less island by means of a sling hung from a helicopter. But they couldn't find a drug strong enough to knock him out.

So the foghorn sounded, and the moose pined away in loneliness. When the mating season was over, he realized his affections had been misplaced and swam home.

You should hear what he says about you. Everyone at the New England Aquarium in Boston talks about Hoover, including Hoover.

Hoover, a spotted harbor seal, has spoken English since the age of 3. By the time he was 11 years old and weighed a roly-poly 260 pounds, he had mastered more than just his name. Visitors are startled by such remarks as, "Come over here" and "How are you?" He speaks in a husky, man's voice and—since he can't make an *R* sound—with a Boston accent.

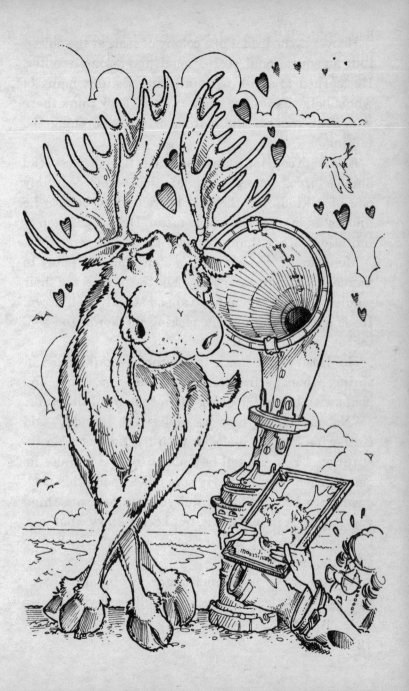

Hoover is the leader of a colony of seals at the aquarium, an educational, recreational, and research center. He learned to speak by mimicking visitors, many of whom believe they are being tricked. They think there is a little man at the bottom of the pool doing the talking.

Although copying human speech is fairly widespread among birds, among mammals, Hoover is definitely one of a kind. Yet there is no reason to believe he understands what the words mean. He is a paragon of imitation rather than a wonder of animal genius.

Members of the aquarium's staff make no effort to increase Hoover's vocabulary. For the purposes of their studies, they want him to go ahead strictly on his own. He is entirely self-taught, picking up words and sentences from the public.

He doesn't talk much in winter. He talks most in spring, when he frequently goes off in a corner and chats with himself, looking up in the air all the while.

"Nobody knows how he makes the sounds," said Katherine Ralls, a zoologist with the Smithsonian Institution. "You can tell he's about to do it because he gets himself organized. He sort of scrunches his neck down into his shoulders, and you can see something wiggling back in his throat, but I don't know what it is. It makes recording easy because we can tell when to stick the mike to him."

No one knows how much more vocabulary Hoover may be able to learn as the years roll by. If you happen to be in Boston, treat yourself to a visit with him. He may greet you with a cheery "Hello, there," or he may toss you a dearly held remark, such as "Get out of here!"

Short in the saddle. Monkeys were banned in 1929 from ever again riding as jockeys at dog-racing tracks in New Jersey.

Iowa bounce. Ever mount a horse from a mile high?

Jim Templeton of Hanlontown, Iowa, did. Or more accurately, he tried.

Templeton sky-dived from a small airplane in 1982. He parachuted 5,500 feet onto a 13-year-old horse named Pinto Bean at a rodeo in Mason City, Iowa.

The promoter of the rodeo insisted that Templeton had set a record by coming down on the horse's back. But some witnesses said the horse either moved or Templeton was wide of the mark. He tumbled off the animal.

Perhaps the daredevil might have done better if he'd tried the feat in the horse latitudes. Or donned horse feathers. No matter. The 3,000 onlookers gave him a loud round of applause.

For love or money. She was young and shy and curved divinely. She was Miss Petunia, and she did it all for charity in 1982. Students at Sunset High School in Miami, Florida, paid to see their favorite teachers kiss her.

Dressed in a fetching black-and-gold gown, Miss Pe-

13

KISSES
1 BUCK

tunia, a 10-week-old piglet, played it cool. She put up with the admiring glances and the kisses, even though she was more at home in a muddy sty.

"She kind of looks like this girl I dated in high school," said Pete Moroney, a woodworking teacher. He closed his eyes before puckering up.

Money from the kiss-a-pig paid for meals for the poor.

The thrill is gone. Tony Stellato of Portland, Oregon, was driving home from work one night in 1982 when he saw a house on fire. He stopped, wondering if anyone was trapped inside.

All of a sudden he heard a woman scream, "My baby! Save my baby!"

Stellato jumped from his car and ran through the open back door. The house was filled with smoke and flames. He began looking for a child—nothing.

Gasping from the smoke, he staggered outside. Above the crackling of the flames he once again heard the cry, "Save my baby!"

Stellato broke through the front door and charged into the burning house again. Desperately, he tried to figure out where the infant might be. Opening the nearest door, he was hit in the face with smoke. That was it—he couldn't see, he couldn't breathe. He fell to the floor and barely made it to the lawn before passing out.

At the Portland Adventist Medical Center he was treated for smoke inhalation. When he was able to speak, he asked about the baby. Was it all right?

15

A nurse told him. The "baby" was a cat. It had escaped uninjured before the woman had started to scream for help.

Future shock. James Lee, an amateur snake collector from Monroe, Louisiana, was feeding a poisonous snake in his home in 1980 as his wife and a neighbor looked on. Lee glanced up to catch a remark, and the snake turned and bit him.

Lee recovered. The snake died.

Get your laundry clean with ivory. A guard at the zoo in Prague, Czechoslovakia, sent a soiled dress shirt to the laundry in 1982. The shirt came back with most of the stains still on it. Rather than throw it away, he wore it to work.

One sweltering day he took off the shirt and carelessly laid it aside. An elephant with a quick eye for a snack gulped it down.

A few days later the shirt came out. The guard washed it and found that the stains were gone. Nature, he announced to newsmen, works better than the laundries of Prague.

Mary, Mary, quite contrary. No one could remember a better-looking racehorse than Sunshine Mary. She stood 16 hands, and her splendid bay coat glistened sleekly. Her brown eyes were clear and alert. Her morning workouts were often a thing of beauty.

Wherever the 3-year-old filly graced Florida race-

tracks—Hialeah, Gulfstream, and Calder—sharp-eyed railbirds noted her form. They dubbed her the loser's loser. In each of her first 10 starts, she finished last.

After 12 races she had outrun just two horses. She broke her string of last place finishes by running tenth in a field of 11 nonwinners, nipping Read For Love in the last stride. The other horse she outplodded, Poca Rosa, was immediately suspended.

Louis B. Underwood, one of Sunshine Mary's trainers, talked of her speed mournfully. "She couldn't beat me in the last eighth of a mile, and I'm seventy-six years old. All she does is sleep and eat."

Absolutely nothing was wrong with her breeding. She was healthy and happy. Yet the more she ran, the slower she ran. In her first race she went to the post a 32–1 long shot and finished last by 25 lengths. The odds on her climbed till they reached 167–1. The bettors had grown wise. Sunshine Mary liked the view from the rear.

"Maybe the reason she's so healthy is that she never ran hard enough to exert herself," said her owner, Jack Root, a retired women's clothier.

The filly was finally banned from Hialeah racetrack. "We refused to accept any more entries from her," declared a state racing official. "She's just cheating the public."

The loser's loser got another chance when the races moved from Hialeah to Calder. In her fourteenth start, she made up 15 lengths in the final ⅜ of a mile and passed 4 horses in a field of 12. It was to be her career best.

Her new trainer, John Valkanet, was encouraged. He entered her next in the first race at Calder on August 31, 1981. Sunshine Mary broke last, began to move up, and suddenly attempted to vault the inside rail. She bounced off it with such force that she was spun halfway around. Landing on her neck, she died almost instantly.

To each her own. A 2-year-old girl was playing outside her house in Yavatmal, India, when she spied a black cobra. As her horrified mother and father watched, the tot grasped the deadly reptile and raised it to her mouth. Before the parents could reach her, she had bitten the snake to death.

SWAT contest. *The Washington Star* held a contest to see who could kill the most houseflies. During the two-week contest, 5,000 children reportedly killed 7 million flies. The $25 first prize was collected by a 13-year-old who, aided by 25 other children, brought in 343,800 dead flies.

Lunch break. It must have been the fastest, if not the smartest, cat in the world that blundered onto a greyhound track in Melbourne, Australia, in 1980.

Officials stopped the race after the cat distracted half of the 8-dog field from chasing the mechanical rabbit. The greyhounds raced after the furry tidbit instead. The cat flashed some nifty footwork of its own and beat them to a hole in the fence.

Whistle while you work. In need of horsemen in 1860, the Pony Express Company advertised for "young, wiry fellows not over 18. Must be expert riders, willing to risk death daily. Orphans preferred."

Clothes call. Should animals be allowed to run around in the nude?

Furthermore, if clothes make the man, what, say, can they do for a cow?

These questions concerned SINA—the Society for Indecency to Naked Animals. The group pledged itself to covering up America's four-legged population.

"All animals," stated SINA, "should wear clothing for the sake of decency; namely, horses, cows, dogs, cats, and other domestic animals that stand higher than four inches or are longer than six inches."

SINA was dreamed up by Alan Abel, a comedy writer, ad man, and producer. It was his way of protesting against "hypocrisy, censorship, and extremism."

The idea was hatched when Abel was driving through Texas in 1955 and found himself in a long line of cars brought to a standstill. A bull and a cow were mating in the middle of the road.

"A woman in the lead car facing me put her head on the steering wheel and covered both ears with her hands," Abel said. "A middle-aged couple behind me looked the other way, pretending not to notice."

Drawing on the experience, Abel wrote a comic short story and sent it off to a magazine. The story was rejected, but three years later, Abel hit the jackpot. He landed SINA on TV. The popular *Today* show aired an interview with SINA's president, "G. Clifford Prout," played by Abel's friend, comedian Buck Henry.

During the program, Prout showed drawings of a cat outfitted in a jump suit, a cow wearing a half-slip, and a horse in Bermuda shorts. Naked animals, he averred, were both a public disgrace and a danger to safety: "They cause accidents on highways when motorists take their eyes off the road . . . and these animals are not grazing; they are hanging their heads in shame!"

An aroused public swamped SINA with letters pro and con. Newspapers from coast to coast seized upon the story. Many of them printed photos of Prout at a children's zoo, contentedly patting a fawn in Madras shorts.

In 1963, Abel couldn't resist picketing the White House. President John Kennedy, his wife, Jackie, and their daughter, Caroline, were pet lovers. Abel marched with a sign asking Jackie to "Clothe Caroline's Horse." Enraged newspapermen hopped upon SINA full-force, dug into its background, and exposed the group as a hoax.

Yet the public refused to dismiss SINA. Nearly 20 years after the White House incident, Abel spoke for 5 hours on New York radio station WOR. The resulting mail shattered all records in the history of the show. People still wanted to believe.

Abel and SINA had accomplished their mission. False values, they had proved, are held dear.

Shooting for par. Golfers at the Taconic Club in Williamstown, Massachusetts, had a complaint in 1934. Their golf balls seemed to disappear into thin air.

Groundskeeper Richard Baxter decided to patrol the course for a day. His patience was rewarded: he spied ten crows flying from the fourth and fifteenth holes, each with a ball in its beak.

Club officials doctored the rules for the tournament that began the next week. It was the first one in history in which players were permitted to carry shotguns.

Friendly persuasion. During the French Revolution, a mob overran the royal palace at Versailles and sought out the keeper of the king's private zoo.

"We have come," announced the leader of the mob, "to free the creatures caged by tyrants!"

"Do as you will," said the keeper, eyeing the rhinoceros. "But don't expect gratitude from every one of the beasts."

The mob had second thoughts and took only the tamer animals.

Playing possum. An angry possum peered out of a letter box at a mailman making his rounds in Front Royal, Virginia, in 1973. Some practical joker had dropped the animal into the box during the night.

The possum passed the time by chewing up about 40 letters before it was rescued. The mailman searched through the litter for return addresses. The writers were advised to try again.

24

As for the possum, it was sent to the outskirts of town without a stamp of approval.

Lassie, why go home? During her engagement at Radio City Music Hall in New York City in 1978, Lassie stayed in a $380-a-day suite at the Plaza Hotel.

The galloping gourmet. A 2-year-old filly named Elizabeth Bolla was a flop as a racehorse till she was introduced to home cooking.

"Lizzie," as she was known among racing folk, belonged to Mrs. Charles Holland, who had purchased the horse in 1928. After a few discouraging races, the owner took young Lizzie off the track.

"Baby horses," Mrs. Holland declared, "have no business running, anyway." For nine months she let Lizzie roam her front yard in New Orleans. Lizzie ate what the family ate.

Returned to the track as a 3-year-old, Lizzie showed what better living can do for a horse. She became a star. By the time she was 5, she had won 20 races out of 49 starts, including 4 in a row.

"Good cooking did it," Mrs. Holland said.

Lizzie was especially fond of spaghetti, chopped beefsteak, and hot dogs. She was willing, however, to settle for coffee, bread, and soda pop in a pinch. When offered anything less, she sulked and refused to run.

Nonscents. In 1980, letter carriers in London, England sprayed their trousers with a chemical that was

supposed to ward off dogs. But no one told the dogs. They didn't object to the foul smell at all. More than 500 postmen were attacked during a 12-month test period. Eight others were clawed by cats, and one was nipped by a crazed squirrel.

The post office abandoned the spray in favor of a simpler method. It launched "Be a Postman's Pal"—a campaign to have dog owners keep their pets indoors when the postman called.

Next time, try a little tenderness. A gray goose was loose on the streets of Lewiston, Idaho, in 1980. It attacked joggers and pedestrians, earning the nickname "mugger goose."

Then it made a mistake. It sank its beak into the wrong man, Dale Litzenberger of the Washington State Game Department. Litzenberger plopped the feathered fiend into a gunnysack and hauled it to a wildlife refuge.

Not so baaad. High winds toppled a 35-foot tree onto a tent at a county fair in Topsfield, Massachusetts, where 125 people were watching a goat-judging contest in 1982. No one was hurt, but two goats fainted.

The goats were brought around by contest officials who gave them mouth-to-mouth resuscitation. "The men are all goat breeders and farmers," explained fair spokesman Warren Rockwell. "They know what to do in these situations."

Deer me. About 500 deer in Iowa had their antlers on backward in the 1980s.

The unfortunate animals were those pictured on yellow deer-crossing signs along the highways. The design

30

was taken from manuals published by the Federal Highway Administration.

"I can imagine some bureaucratic artist in Washington drawing a deer and never having seen one in his life," fumed Ron Avenson, an Iowa state representative and a hunter.

It only works in Tuskaloosa. Kham Saeng of Bangkok, Thailand, bought a 40-year-old elephant in 1981. He expected to make money from people who believed that walking under an elephant brings good luck.

The elephant did bring luck to Saeng—all of it bad. While the huge beast was quietly waiting for a customer, a mischievous boy gave its tail a sharp yank.

Down the street went the elephant in a frenzy. It smashed two houses, wrecked several market stalls, and trampled the fence at the home of an army general.

As lawsuits piled up to his chin, Saeng said that he was no longer sure about the tradition of elephants bringing good luck.

Elementary equine. Curly Smith, a horse, received a diploma from York Grade School in Idaho in 1939. Curly had carried children of the H. M. Smith family to the school for 12 years without missing a day.

Natural gas. "Burping cows must rank as the number-one source of air pollution in the U.S.," states the Environmental Protection Agency. According to the

31

agency, "Ten cows burp enough gas in a year to provide all the space-heating, water-heating, and cooking requirements of a small house."

The night has a thousand eyes. Jody Gerard, 12, had the state of New York squirming.

During the summer of 1978 Jody sold worms to fishermen in Eddyville, New York. He crept on his hands and knees with a flashlight on rainy nights to nab the muddy night crawlers. His "red wigglers" sold for 35 cents a dozen. A jar of them cost 55 cents.

Then, in 1979, the state sank its hooks into his backyard business. It advised him that he owed 64 cents in taxes. Moreover, if he didn't apply for a sales tax license within 30 days, he would be taken to court and sued.

His mother remembered the moment. "He was sitting at the table eating breakfast," she said, "and I was going through the mail. I saw this letter and I said, 'Jody, here's a letter for you.' He opened it and almost died! He had visions of them taking away his boat and motor."

Jody was earning about a dollar a day selling worms. The most his mother could remember him making on a very good day was two dollars. His small homemade sign at the foot of the driveway attracted a few local fishermen. General Motors his business was not.

Jody immediately sent the state 64 cents for the taxes. "The check cost me fifty cents," his mother said.

When his case hit the newspapers, a sympathetic public rallied behind him. He received about $80 from supporters as far away as Switzerland.

The New York legislature was embarrassed by the outcry. After doing a bit of wiggling, it passed the "worm law" in 1980. Children under 18 were spared from paying taxes on businesses that brought in less than $600 a year.

Jody was pleased and relieved. He looked forward to "not being famous anymore."

Don't know why, I just do. In 1981, a Chinese village had a mule that couldn't kick the smoking habit. It did kick people, however, when it didn't get a puff or two.

If someone blew cigarette smoke into its nostrils, the mule became a willing worker. Otherwise, it wouldn't budge. It kicked or bit 16 villagers over a period of three years.

The mule's mother had died when it was two days old. Thereafter it was cared for by a man who smoked so much he was called "Big Chimney."

Despite its bad habits, the villagers withheld the name of the mule from the outside world (no, it wasn't "Smokey the Mule"). They understood. . . .

As an ancient Chinese philosopher said, "The world would be a far better place if people did the work and mules did the smoking."

Wiggle, waggle, waddle. Players at the Lakeview Golf Course in Omaha, Nebraska, never quite got used to J.R. the duck. She stood quietly as they swung, never uttering a quack of approval or disapproval. But her stare, which seemed to note mistakes of form, could be unnerving.

"It was eerie," a golfer said. "I was putting on the

sixth green, and I felt a presence. I looked around, and there was this duck watching me."

J.R. arrived at her career by chance. She was given to a family as a gag. After she had grown up, the family freed her on the golf course. They visited her once a month.

"J.R. chose people over other ducks because she spent all of her early life with people," explained Dallas Wendt, the course pro. "She was treated well and learned to trust people. She never did trust other ducks. She laid many eggs but never became a mother."

Every morning J.R. showed up at the first tee to select partners. She normally logged six or seven holes before returning to the clubhouse. After a short rest, she went out for another round. Occasionally she waddled a full nine holes. She preferred women but accompanied men as a last resort.

For a year and a half, J.R. was a fixture at the course. She was killed by a golf ball in 1983, having followed the game to the end.

Don't let this rattle you. At the 1980 National Rattlesnake Sacking Championships, Cotton Dillard, of Brownwood, Texas, claimed he held the world's rattlesnake lifting record. He said he had once hoisted 450 rattlers—all of them wound around his torso, neck, and arms—at one time.

The record seems untouchable. Or would you care to try?

36

The only one who didn't vote for himself. Scott, a 15-year-old mutt, drew only four write-in votes in the 1982 election for mayor of Cumberland, Maryland. He placed far behind the winner, George Wyckoff, Jr., who received 3,879 votes. Still, Scott defeated three human candidates who received fewer votes.

Next time, throw rice. A carrier pigeon was seized on a window ledge in Tel Aviv, Israel, in 1980. Taped to one leg was a note in Arabic.

The note was rushed to police. Detectives feared it was meant for Arab terrorists planning to blow up buildings in the city.

The pigeon created a flutter of front-page headlines while Israeli code experts went to work. Their conclusion: The bird was no stool pigeon. The note was an ancient Arab proverb wishing good luck to a pair of newlyweds.

Cat-ch as cat-ch can. After large numbers of rats had shorted out Peking's subway system several times in the 1970s, China's *People's Daily* called upon the public to keep more cats.

Turntail. A tiger escaped from its cage at the Washington Park Zoo in Milwaukee in 1931. The animal leaped upon a painter and had the man down when an attendant charged over and swung a left hook to the snout. While the tiger was taking a nine-count, the attendant seized a scraper belonging to the painter and swung again. The tiger blinked, belched, and fled back into its cage.

For a stable economy. Most Americans never heard of the dark horse in the 1980 Presidential election in which Ronald Reagan defeated Jimmy Carter. He had but one name, Butterscotch.

Butterscotch's campaign manager, Dr. Dorothy Magallon, of Louisville, Kentucky, thought the best way to solve the nation's problems was to put a horse in the driver's seat. Butterscotch, a Palomino gelding that drove a customized red Lincoln Continental around her farm, was a natural choice.

The Butterscotch for President campaign started as pure fun but soon caught on with the public. Magallon said that at least one voter survey, the Gallop Poll, had her candidate ahead.

Campaign funds never amounted to a sack of oats, but slogans were plentiful. Among them were: "Keep a tight rein on the economy"; "Don't put the Cart(er) before the horse"; and "We've had no sense and nonsense—now it's time for horse sense."

Despite making a good run, Butterscotch was defeated on Election Day. He became quite downhearted over the voting, until he got in with some of his bucking horse friends from the rodeo. They apparently reminded him that this was not the first time a horse had lost out to a cowboy.

Added event. A swarm of bees attacked hundreds of schoolgirls at a track meet in Vereeniging, South

40

Africa, in 1979. The bees were believed to have been driven into a mad passion by the girls' hair spray.

Or were they honey blonds?

Just a dreamer, but aren't we all? In 1975, an orangutan came to a riverbank near Djakarta, Indonesia, but not for a drink of water. It dashed up to a woman who was undressing to bathe and smacked her with a kiss.

The woman screamed and fainted dead away. The orangutan darted back into the jungle.

Cold duck. Warren Stovell, a Louisiana hunter, shot two ducks in 1980 and stored them in the freezer. He planned to have them mounted.

When he opened the freezer that evening, out flew one of the ducks and it flapped around the floor. Stovell screamed in alarm.

"He thought the duck had come back to get him," said his wife.

After the duck had warmed up, Stovell showed he was warmhearted, too. He rewarded the plucky creature by shipping it off to a duck farm rather than to a taxidermist.

Flat feet on the front line. Alexander the Great didn't think much of elephants as tanks of war. But Seleucus, one of his successors, liked them. Seleucus traded Afghanistan for 500 of the huge beasts.

Second nature. On May 16, 1981, in the fifth race at Hialeah, Florida, Sir Wimbledon showed the form that made him somewhat famous. The 3-year-old colt finished second for the *ninth straight time*.

Twenty lengths away from the lead, Sir Wimbledon charged up to second entering the home stretch. "He

43

was flying until he saw only one horse left in front of him," said Don Ball, his trainer. "Then he stopped himself."

Turf and surf. Chris Nelson and Harry Hansen glimpsed two pairs of antlers off to their right. Nothing new about that. Countless hunters had glimpsed antlers earlier that day in 1931. Only Nelson and Hansen weren't hunters.

They were lobster fishermen.

And they were standing in their boat in the Atlantic Ocean off the New Jersey coast.

They shook their heads and looked again. No, the sun wasn't playing tricks with their eyesight. Antlers moved above the calm ocean—deer, swimming at 2 knots an hour.

The fishermen swung into action. Humming a mixture of sea tunes and cowboy ballads, they hastily fashioned lariats out of anchor ropes and pointed the boat toward the swimmers.

"Ahoy, there!" bellowed Nelson.

"Yippee!" Hansen whooped like a cowboy.

The two deer were heading nowhere but toward exhaustion. After ramming the boat, they gave up the struggle and were lassoed. Nelson and Hansen hauled them aboard with the lobsters and roped their legs.

Some old salts gawked as the catch arrived at the dock. They couldn't have been more amazed had the two fishermen unloaded a couple of mermaids.

The deer were turned loose in the woods near Free-

hold. What had driven them so far out in the ocean was never explained.

Get me to the zoo on time. If it had rained, the wedding would have been for the birds. But a clear day it was, and so Jody Sussman and Kurt Metzger didn't have to get married inside the bird house at the Cincinnati Zoo.

They exchanged vows outdoors in front of the gorillas.

"We both have a tremendous love for animals and wanted to be married in a place that means most to us," said the groom. "That's the zoo. I think it's great to get married in front of gorillas. I prefer them as wedding guests over a lot of people I know."

Crushed leather. When President William Taft, who weighed more than 300 pounds, was in the Philippines, he cabled Secretary of War Elihu Root, "Took a long horseback ride today. Feeling fine."

Root cabled back, "How is the horse?"

Positively electrifying. Sedgewick the cat used up one of his nine lives at a power station in Cambridge, England, in 1981. He got stuck in a generator and blacked out half the city.

Somehow Sedgewick survived the 30,000-volt shock, but he limped away looking like a burned bedroom slipper.

Don't get around much anymore. You can fool some

of the pigeons all of the time—at least in Winston-Salem, North Carolina.

A band of pesky pigeons flew around workers remodeling the Center for the Performing Arts in 1983. So the hard-pressed workers set up a line of defense. They hung six-foot plastic snakes from the roof.

The pigeons approached the building, saw the "snakes," and did a U-turn.

Donder, Blitzen, and Sitzbath. The stress of modern life is giving even reindeer ulcers.

In 1980, Dr. Claes Rehbinder studied reindeer that had been slaughtered in the Lapp villages of northern Sweden. An amazing four-fifths of the animals suffered from ulcers.

The stomach bleeding was attributed to nervous exhaustion brought on by modern machinery. In earlier days, the Lapps herded animals by skiing beside them and singing soothing melodies. Now the Lapps use snowmobiles, motorcycles, and helicopters. The noise upsets the animals.

The Lapps have not been asked to return to skis. But there is concern that the quality of reindeer meat may be affected by the noise. And *that* could cause more stress, certainly among people who pay fancy prices for the meat.

High-wire act. In 1939, George Stofflet was minding his own business outside his home in Reading, Pennsylvania, when he was nearly kayoed by a fish. A 12-inch

trout, already fried, dropped from the sky and landed at his feet.

The trout had wiggled loose from the clutches of a heron flying overhead. On the way down, it struck a high-tension wire. Stofflet had a picture taken of himself holding the fish, crisply fried by 66,000 volts.

II.

Man's Best Friends

Hold still, please. After General Zachary Taylor became President, his horse, Old Whitey, was pastured on the White House lawn. Visitors yanked hairs from his tail for souvenirs.

A chip off the old block. In the Hough's Neck section of Quincy, Massachusetts, drivers once stopped for the world's only "Louis Crossing."

The sign was nailed to a lamp post because Louis, a 9-year-old basset hound, loved chocolate-chip cookies. Daily, he risked his life and limb by crossing the road to get to the other side—where stores sold the cookies he craved. The square sign, tipped like a baseball diamond, warned drivers to beware. Louis's picture ap-

peared below the word CAUTION and above LOUIS CROSSING.

His owner not only arranged for the sign in 1981 but also set up charge accounts to make Louis's life as a chocoholic lawful.

Homespun. It is said that Mrs. John Quincy Adams kept silkworms for pets. They fed on mulberry leaves and repaid the First Lady by spinning silk for her gowns.

Chow chow. Veterinarian Ben Willis didn't know what to think when Steve and Sandra Stewart brought their tiny Boston terrier puppy, Sweetie Pie, to his animal hospital in Marianna, Florida, in 1981. The dog had thrown up several pennies and wouldn't eat.

Willis operated.

"I've taken everything out of dogs from corncobs, nuts, bottle nipples, rubber stoppers, bones, needles with thread—you name it," Willis said. "But I've never seen or heard of anything to compare with this."

From Sweetie Pie's stomach came 80 cents in coins, a piece of lead the size of a quarter, a staple, and a metal shoe from a Monopoly game. The 3½-pound puppy had been carrying around half a pound of metal —one-seventh of its body weight!

Hurry on down. Danny was standing on the roof of a 14-story building under construction in 1980. His master, Herman Dean, whistled to him from the ground floor.

Danny took the most direct route down—a 140-foot leap into a pile of mud. For a moment the 7-year-old dog lay without moving. Then he struggled up and limped around on a sore leg, his only injury.

Dean, a building inspector in New Carrollton, Virginia, had thought Danny was on the ground floor when he whistled. "I just couldn't believe my eyes," he said. "I thought he was dead."

Where did Danny learn to respond to a whistled command? At an obedience school?

"I trained him myself," Dean said. "I guess I trained him pretty good."

Living high. Lady Beaverbrook, widow of the English newspaper tycoon, traveled in style. Once she was told that her dog must be kept in a separate compartment on the flight from Britain to Canada. No way, she said, and chartered an airliner just for herself and her dog.

Muzzle tov. When a New York mutt named Greggie "Lump Lump" Taylor reached the age of 13 in 1982, she celebrated in style. Four hundred pets were invited to her "bark mitzvah."

But we never talked much. When President John Tyler's horse died, he was buried with the inscription: "Here lies the body of my good horse, The General. For years he bore me around the circuit of my practice, and all that time he never made a blunder. Would that his master could say the same—John Tyler."

Little things mean a lot. Charles Baudelaire, a nineteenth-century French poet, cut quite a figure strolling the boulevards of Paris with his companion—a lobster on a leash.

Meow mansion. Ernest Hemingway, one of America's greatest writers, kept so many pet cats on his estate in Cuba that he had to build a special guest house for them.

Paperweight. A lady who took home delivery of the *Dallas Morning News* had a complaint. The newspaper had become too big and heavy. Her well-trained little dog could no longer fetch it into the house.

A spokesman for the newspaper politely suggested she get herself a bigger dog.

Hold the catsup. Skerry the cat lived in luxury and ate steak. After her owner died, she didn't have to worry about where her next T-bone was coming from. She inherited $100 a week for life.

The 14-year-old alley cat belonged to Jean Gordon of London, England, who died in 1981. Part of Gordon's $250,000 estate was set aside for Skerry's care, including a lifetime supply of steaks, medium rare.

Dogging the politicians. President Warren Harding's beloved Laddie Boy led a dog's life with style. Not only did the Airedale have his own private valet, but he also sat in at Cabinet meetings on his special chair. He listened quietly to the debates, neither okaying decisions with a wag of his tail nor objecting with a toothy grumble.

Laddie Boy was probably the only American dog to be asked his thoughts on matters of state. The July 17,

1921, issue of *The Washington Star* printed a fanciful "interview" that covered nearly an entire page and was illustrated with two cartoons.

The reporter had Laddie Boy "voice" his opinions on a range of subjects. The leading figure of dogdom lashed out against the ban on Mexican hairless dogs and against the use of mail-sled dogs in Alaska. He requested that the Secretary of Agriculture look into the quality of dog biscuits, and he expressed the hope that every watchdog in the nation would be granted an eight-hour workday.

The questions were put with mock seriousness, and the "answers" were recorded in the same fashion.

Now 'ear this. Bingo, a young bulldog, had a sore ear in 1934. His owner, Mrs. Edward P. Thomas of Frederick, Maryland, took him to Dr. R. V. Smith.

A week later she telephoned the doctor. Bingo's ear was well, she said. The owner couldn't understand how one treatment could be so effective.

"One treatment?" exclaimed the doctor. "Why, Bingo has been a patient at my office every day this week."

The puppy had visited his office at the same time every day, leaping onto the table, and lying quietly until treated. After the treatment was over, he would jump down and trot home. When the ear healed, Bingo stopped running to the doctor.

A poultry pace. No runner drew more looks of disbe-
58

lief than Wilbur, who liked to turkey trot . . . er . . . jog on the streets of Dousman, Wisconsin, in 1982. He always ran behind Bob Fecteau.

"Wilbur kept right up with me," Fecteau said proudly of his 25-pound pet turkey. "He even tried to pass me sometimes."

Don't expect me to be everyone's friend. When business was slow, Stephan Dunstan of New York City occasionally took Paddy for a ride in his taxi cab. Paddy, a friend's pet pig, was a porker with personality.

One Saturday in 1929, Paddy looked pale and wan. Dunstan drove him uptown for some air. At 129th Street, he stopped for a traffic light. Someone noticed his passenger, and a crowd gathered. There was laughter. Paddy didn't fancy being the object of ridicule. He snorted his feelings with feeling.

The laughing and snorting grew as the crowd grew. Traffic stopped. A policeman handed Dunstan a summons. Vainly, the cabbie protested that Paddy, the big ham, had caused the trouble.

In court the following Monday, Dunstan grunted guilty to a charge of disorderly conduct and paid a $1 fine.

Blue ribbon grapes. Sir Joshua Reynolds, the English portrait painter, had a pet macaw that frequently tried to eat the painted grapes in his pictures. The macaw prompted Reynolds to comment that "birds and beasts were as good judges of pictures as men are."

First, wash your hands. Josephine, empress of the
French, owned an orangutan that sat at her dinner
table in a coat.

You ain't seen mutton yet. Mary had a little lamb, but it merely followed her to school one day. Lisa Bernard, 16, had a lamb that paid her way through college.

The lamb, named Shelty, was the prize at a high-stakes livestock auction at the 1982 Midwinter Fair in Imperial, California. No ordinary lamb chop, Shelty was the Supreme Champion Suffolk lamb. She was in perfect shape for the sale. Lisa had risen before dawn each morning to walk her and make sure there wasn't much fat under the wool.

Shelty was bought by Loren Sheppard of the Guy Packing Company after a bidding war. The price at the auction started at $10 a pound—$2 below the record set at the fair the previous year—and quickly zoomed past $50.

The wealthiest bidders "were using their millions against me," Sheppard said. "I just thought I'd see how far they'd go."

How far was nearly out of sight. But Sheppard stayed the route. His winning bid for the 113-pound Shelty was a record $550 a pound.

That figures out to $62,150!

Lisa's parents said the money would be put aside for her college education. Lisa, a shy girl, was nearly speechless.

Winning bidders in other years often barbecued the grand champion at a party. A kinder fate awaited Shelty. She was used as breeding stock.

Locks are for the birds. Harry Houdini, the famous

escape artist, had a parrot, Pat Houdini, for a stage companion. Pat learned to pick locks while watching his master fascinate audiences. When Houdini died, the parrot lived with Mrs. Houdini in California.

When Mrs. Houdini traveled to the East in 1938, she left Pat at a boarding home for pets but forgot to tell the staff about his ability to pick locks.

As soon as the coast was clear, Pat picked the lock to his cage. He disappeared into the Hollywood hills, singing as he soared to freedom.

And in the mane ballroom, too. A lock from the mane of General Robert E. Lee's horse, Traveler, was auctioned in New York's Waldorf–Astoria Hotel in 1981. It sold for $110.

Have trunk, will travel. Can an elephant who likes to wreck things ever find true happiness?

Slim Lewis, an animal trainer, had an elephant named Tuska. If Tuska went too long without exercise, he became cranky and wrecked his quarters.

By 1932 Lewis had all he could take. In desperation he rented Tuska out to a house-wrecking company in Seattle. On his first job, the elephant teamed with a truck to topple a house from its concrete foundation.

Tuska had found happiness.

It's a sin to tell a lie. Members of 60 Maryland families were asked the question, "Who in the family gets the most touches, words, and smiles?"

Forty-four percent answered: the family pet.

Double-talk. Birds of all kinds were popular in ancient Rome. When Octavian returned to Rome after vanquishing Marc Antony, he was supposed to have been presented with a raven trained to say, "Hail, Octavian, victorious leader."

Octavian was so delighted that he rewarded the trainer handsomely. But a jealous bystander made the trainer admit that he had coached *another* raven to say, "Hail, Antony, victorious leader," just in case Antony won. The amused Octavian made the trainer share his reward with the informer.

Heel, eel. Crassus, one of the richest men in ancient Rome, had a moray eel that came to him when he called, and also took food from his hand. He was so fond of it that he decked it out in earrings and other jewelry. He wept when it died.

Armed forces petwork. After Rhodesia's civil war ended in 1980, Norman Travers revealed that he had successfully defended his home with a fearsome troop of animals.

Travers and his wife, Jill, ran a 300-acre tobacco farm in Wedza. Theirs was the only farm to escape attacks during the war.

Commander of the home guard was Cassius the lion, who had free range of the farm. Cassius was backed up by a leopard who leaped onto the shoulders of visitors; by Dudley the warthog, who tore apart furniture with his tusks; and by a crocodile who defended the swimming pool.

The Traverses also had a pet vulture, a noncombatant. It rapped on the dining room window with its beak at mealtimes.

Outfoxed. Milutin Stojin, a Bulgarian farmer, found a fox cub in 1979 and trained it as a watchdog. The sly fox bided its time for a year—till Stojin left it in charge of the farm while he went into town. When Stojin returned, he learned that you can take an animal out of the wild but not the wild out of the animal. All of his 200 chickens were slain, and the fox was gone.

Sheeping on the job. President Woodrow Wilson put a small flock of sheep to trimming the White House lawn during World War I, thus relieving men for battle.

The woolly, self-propelled landscape artists drew bad notices. They cut the grass, but they also ate the shrubs and beds of flowers. Mrs. Wilson defended the animals from citizens who felt the White House had been clipped of dignity.

As the sheep multiplied, they attracted crowds of children. A favorite of the kids was Old Ike, a ram that chewed tobacco and had a special weakness for cigar butts.

Windbroken. Goggles for dogs were the rage in London during the 1920s. Thousands of pairs were sold to motorists who took their pets on trips in open cars.

A course with four dog legs. One of America's finest hunting dogs never won a field trial, but he knew his business. Smokey, a mixed poodle, retrieved so many golf balls that his master didn't have to buy a ball for nearly 10 years.

Every day Smokey searched a wooded, out-of-bounds area near the golf course alongside the home of his owner, Bob Ticehurst, in Wildwood, Florida. Once the little gray pooch recovered 35 balls in an hour.

What's more, Smokey always obeyed the rules. He never snatched a ball from a rough or a fairway.

Walk on. Richard Martin didn't have a pet to enter in the 1939 Boys' Club of New York pet show. So on the way he picked up a stray cat in the street. It won a blue ribbon.

The back of my foot to you. Animals, like humans, can have identity crises. That means they don't know who they are.

Mort the rabbit probably thought he was a mule. He certainly kicked like one. His hind-leg action made him the terror of Alex Lindsay's backyard in Spokane, Washington, in 1934. He never dodged a fight.

Yet for a time his fame was merely local. Word of his prowess didn't spread outside the neighborhood until he took on Rex, a police dog, in an over-the-weight match.

Perhaps Rex thought to have some fun. Perhaps he came into the yard to straighten out the mean, mixed-

up little rabbit. It made no difference. The fight was no contest.

Rex showed his teeth.

Mort showed his tail. Then he let fly with his hind legs, catching the dog squarely on the nose. Rex became a believer on the spot and beat a hasty retreat.

Thereafter the yard was known far and wide as "Mort's Fort."

III.

Sales and Services

Pulling the wool over your ears. The hottest item on British radios and jukeboxes in 1982 was the nursery rhyme "Baa Baa Black Sheep." It was sung without words by a chorus of sheep.

Record-producer Richard Branson dreamed up the novelty. His aunt grazed a flock of 600 black Welsh mountain sheep, and Branson noticed that the sheep bleated in many tones. Test recordings of the flock showed that it was simply a matter of selecting the bleats that fit the melody.

The flip side of the record was "Rock Around the Flock."

Every cat should have one. You say you want to build a scratching post for your cat? Well, it helps to have a guide.

So lay your hands on *Building Furniture for Your Cat,* one of 3,000 booklets, newsletters, and reports published by the state of Wisconsin in 1981.

Everything you've always wanted. Neiman-Marcus, the Dallas department store, takes pride in its selection of merchandise, which "will meet every taste, every occasion, and every price." Among the more gleefully peddled items: electric blankets for pet lions and umbrellas for dogs.

A barkler alarm. Are you worried about burglars when you're away from home?

Do you feel that you can't trust leaving the lights on or the radio playing?

Or maybe you don't like bars on your windows?

Your worries may be over. You can buy tapes and records of dogs barking. They're made to scare off burglars.

Paul Indianer, founder of Dog Alarm of Perrine, Florida, got the idea when he heard a policeman talk about the best way to keep criminals from breaking into a house. It is the sound of barking dogs.

Not everyone wants to own a dog and put up with the mess, the odor, the fleas, and the vet's bills. So how about a recording?

"Anyone can tape dogs barking," Indianer said, "but it sounds like a tape." He achieved a realistic effect by putting two attack Doberman pinschers in a recording studio.

"We got six minutes of a wide variety of dog sounds

—barks, growls, and snarls," he said. His tape was packaged with a nine-page booklet of crime-fighting tips and two signs that read, WARNING, THESE PREMISES ARE GUARDED BY ATTACK DOGS.

Should you have the kind of record or tape player that can repeat automatically, the sounds can guard your home for hours, even days.

One suggestion: Don't play your watch record too loud. It might fake out burglars, but your neighbors may visit you with a shotgun.

Now here is one you haven't herd. Human thieves aren't the only ones to be fooled by recordings.

In northern California sheep farmers discovered that hymn singing makes coyotes nervous. So the farmers tucked recordings of gospel music in the midst of their flocks. However, if the machine is left on for long periods, the coyotes grow used to it. Once they decide they have nothing to fear, there go the sheep. Coyotes are smart and growing smarter in their battle to survive.

Sheep ranchers across the West were desperate enough to try anything in their losing war with the coyotes. At first they spread the poison 1080. That was outlawed by President Nixon. Then they tried recordings of dogs howling. The coyotes figured that one out fast. Coyotes become upset by anything that reminds them of man. Howling dogs just reminded them of howling dogs.

When the coyotes eventually wise up to hymn singing, the ranchers may have to try opera.

I'll walk behind you. Does your dog have everything but is afraid someone might take it away? Not to worry. In 1983, the first bullet-proof dog vest was introduced.

The pooch protector was a lightweight coat that covered the dog's back—and it cost $400. It was also waterproof and fireproof, claimed the manufacturer, Production Versatility Limited of Dorset, England.

Signs of the times. For those of you who want protection but no noise, how about a sign that reads, THIS HOUSE PATROLLED BY AN ATTACK TURTLE?

Jerry and Maureen Padulo of Arlington Heights, Illinois, a suburb of Chicago, started a business called Wacky Signs. The humorous warnings frighten off burglars and save them from being ripped by a rabbit, torn by tropical fish, dropped by a duck, or captured by a crab.

There are a number of other wacky signs announcing the presence of attack animals such as guinea pigs, hamsters, boa constrictors, birds, and all sorts of small dogs, including puppies.

Naturally, there is a sign for an attack housewife.

"That was our first one," Padulo said.

Trouble in paradise. Not all alarms are aimed at burglars.

Would you believe one that was meant to scare off weak-willed fatties? The alarm oinked like a pig whenever the refrigerator door swung open.

The Refrigerator Oinkolater sold for $14.85 when it

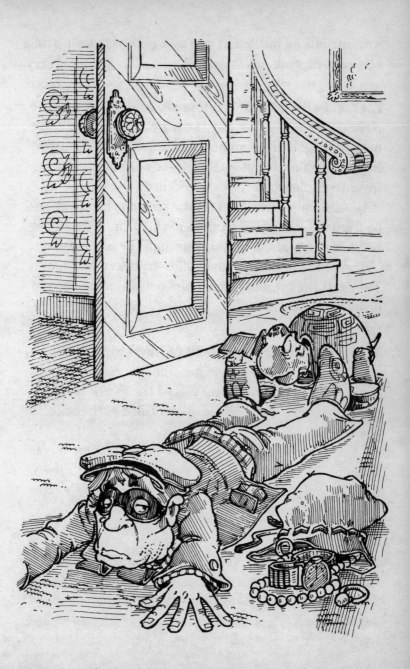

was introduced in 1982. It was guaranteed to keep dieters from pigging out in peace.

Lights, bells, action. Winters are cold in Brownville, Nebraska. One bitter day, Lorin F. Soward couldn't hear his dog, Benji, scraping on the door to come inside. Right then Soward vowed to remedy the situation. He invented a doorbell for cats and dogs.

His animal doorbell is a plastic scratch plate that can be fixed to either or both sides of the door. When a pet paws at the plate, a battery-run light or bell is set off.

The lights and bells have different colors and tones. They tell the owner whether the pet wants to come in or go out.

What, you never saw a field of blackbirds? A store in Wilkes-Barre, Pennsylvania, had a load of unsold birdseed in 1982. The owner placed the following newspaper ad offering the birdseed at a third of the regular price.

"You'll never believe this, but it's true. Our buyer thought if he planted the seed, he'd grow robins, finches, and bluebirds. We'd like to plant him. We have tons of wild birdseed we'd rather not have. . . ."

Eau de skunk. Ray Hanson's company, Skunks Unlimited, did a runaway business selling Super Skunk. That was the trade name for what he termed plain old "skunk stink."

A professional trapper in Cumberland, Wisconsin, Hanson caught skunks, drugged them to sleep, and withdrew the fluid from their odor sacks with a hypodermic needle. The fluid was weakened, bottled, and sold to hunters as a liquid or a gel.

The product was used to hide human scent, improving the hunter's chances for success. The stuff was supposed to be spread on the ground and shrubbery near the hunter. The skunk odor then carried downwind to the prey. But some customers forgot to read the directions and rubbed Super Skunk on their clothing. Goodbye, clothes; hello, loneliness!

"I always bottled it outdoors on a breezy day," Hanson said. "When I was done, I took a long shower and removed the smell. After bottling, I never planned on going anywhere for the next few days."

Did Hanson's wife Marge object to his keeping company with skunks?

"No, he was real careful when he was bottling. The smell was pretty well gone when he was through," she said. "He taught us that skunks smell like money."

Hot tub. A company in Cedar Rapids, Iowa, made a small electric heater for birdbaths. A coil warmed the water to about 45° F so that the birds could clean themselves during the winter.

It also made tasty chicken soup.

T'anks a lot. A study conducted by scientists at the University of Pennsylvania found that fish have a

calming effect on people. Students living in a room with a fish tank were not as prone to anxiety as other students.

But most people don't want to spend the time cleaning up fish tanks. Or worry about keeping tropical fish alive. In 1982, Fish Video One offered an easy substitute.

A television tape, Fish Video One showed rare fish swimming in blue waters, complete with the sound of bubbles. All you had to do was pop the tape into your video cassette recorder and turn on your TV set. Presto! The screen lit up with fish, the first one-hour TV show that didn't get on your nerves.

Or need cleaning up.

Cat-apulting the dice. The first board game for bored cats was called Mr. Meow. It crept onto the market in 1981.

Two can play, a human and a feline. The players each use a plastic marker that advances around the game board with the roll of the dice. Points are added and subtracted for landing on certain squares. The winner is the first player with 30 mouse points.

To play, the cat has to be in the ready position with front paws outstretched. The dice are placed on the cat's front paws and the cat flips them.

Only an understanding owner, however, will know if the cat is in the purr-fect mood to play.

Putting on the dog. Frank Temel didn't invent a car

that can go from Maine to California on a single gallon of gas. Or a television set that never needs repairing.

He invented a dog-and-cat toilet.

Temel, of Boca Raton, Florida, believed that it was about time that dogs quit using lawns. His toilet is a stall with a floor of aluminum slats. Below the floor are spray nozzles and a tank of water. On two sides are pipes and hoses. When the dog (or cat) steps off, a motor turns the floor upside down, and the slats are sprayed clean.

"I'm a hero now," said Temel, who once considered himself a disgrace to his family. "Everybody loves me."

Yoga bare. Shigenori Masuda, of Tokyo, Japan, taught cats and dogs how to relax—by practicing yoga.

He got the idea while he was doing yoga exercises in 1974, and noticed his poodle acting strangely.

"I suddenly realized he was trying to copy me," Masuda said.

The first yoga position pets learned was to lie on the floor with their legs stretched out. The positions became more complex as they were able to bend themselves to gain the greatest amount of relaxation.

Old folks at home. Gretchen Scanlan had a vision in 1978: a retirement home for dogs and cats.

Older people worry about what will happen to their pets after they're gone. So she decided to offer them peace of mind. The result was Kent's Retirement Home for Pets. Located in a ranch-style house on two acres, it overlooks the Peconic Bay in Riverhead, New York.

For a one-time fee, the animals have the run of the house, plus a fenced play area outside. A live-in couple acts as foster parents, so to speak, and provides lifetime care for retirees.

New bird in the sky. Advice to farmers whose crops are being eaten by birds: Go fly a kite.

Some 150 farmers in California flew kites with hawks painted on them in 1983. Each kite was suspended in the sky by a helium balloon. The space-age scarecrows seemed to fool the birds.

Come and get it. Soup kitchens provide food for hungry, jobless men and women. The Animal Charity, in Youngstown, Ohio, went two legs better. The organization started the first free food service for pets only.

"If you have to choose between feeding your kids and feeding your animal, most people pick their kids," said Edward Goist, a director of the charity.

So in the hard times of 1982, the charity began passing out dog and cat food to needy pet owners.

Call in sick on Monday. David Laidlaw of Redford Township, Michigan, was sitting around one day in 1980 looking at his collie, King, and decided that pets needed a union.

Laidlaw and three friends formed United Pets of America, local 738 (that's PET on the phone dial). The UPA started with seven members, all dogs. Any pet, however, could join.

"We gave them rights and everything," Laidlaw said.

The UPA maintained that dogs with two years' seniority should not be fed dry food two days in a row. Moreover, "management" had to advise pets of vacations one week in advance.

Although it was a spoof, the union was organized in a professional manner. For three dollars in dues, pets received a registration slip, certificate of membership, and a union charter book. The charter was drawn up at the UPA's first convention in—where else?—Paw Paw, Michigan.

One question: If the pets walked off the job, would you call it a wildcat strike?

Now don't wolf it down. In 1972, Gloria Lissner of Chicago started Happy Tails, a pet-grooming shop. In the clothing department, dogs could be decked out in tuxedos, pajamas, silk robes, and suits made to measure.

Ten years later Lissner branched out into pet food. She opened the doors of the nation's first dog delicatessen. At her Famous Fido's Doggie Deli, dogs ate high off the hog. Their owners looked into glass showcases at natural foods shaped like the real thing—steak, pot pies, frosted pupcakes, and more. Snacks or complete meals could be purchased frozen, to go, or gobbled on the spot. High-class canines dined restaurant style: Food was served to them in bowls set on little white tables with napkins and a vase of flowers.

Just add a little uncontaminated water. A mail-order company in Van Nuys, California, developed a dog food that could be stored for use in the event of a disaster.

"A lot of people wouldn't want to abandon their pets," said Gene Tarman, president of Country Roads Survival Products.

The dehydrated chow, with a wheat-and-meat base, cost $23.75 for a six-can case in 1981. It was called Sir Vival. (Get it?)

The company had a problem developing a flavor that cats like.

Open wide, please. In Scotland they put braces on sheep.

Farmers don't care about pretty smiles. The thin strips of stainless steel are strictly for profit.

Ewes (female sheep) in Scotland munch tough food such as turnips or heather. Loose-toothed ewes often develop Broken Mouth. Their teeth break off or fall out, making it difficult to chew. Such sheep usually are sold for slaughter and bring a lower price than if they had a few more years of eating and lambing in them. (Rams, being more expensive, are fed a gentler diet and never see a dentist.)

The braces require about a minute to put on. They bind wobbly teeth to well-rooted ones.

United they stand!

I now pronounce you mutt and mate. Barry Sum-

mers, a Chicago pastor, performed wedding ceremonies for dogs, cats, and other animals. His services included flowers and a three-tiered wedding cake.

Creature comforts. The San Diego Zoo began providing its dogs and big cat population with heated water beds in 1983.

The first water bed went to a Chinese wild dog, also known as a dhole. The clever dog pretended to be pregnant. She wasn't but she got to keep the bed, anyway.

Jill, an Indochinese leopard that actually was pregnant, received the second water bed. She liked it so well that she dragged her food onto it. She thought it was her den.

The beds are thin hides of flexible aluminum filled with water, and weigh about 100 pounds. The claws of tigers can't pierce the material, and the beds can be washed with a hose. Covered with hay, they are kept at 75° to 80° F and are especially good for warming baby animals on chilly nights.

Moo light becomes you. Scientists in Cambridge, England, have taught cows and sheep to switch lights on and off.

The lessons began after animal lovers accused farmers of being cruel to livestock by keeping them indoors under hot lights.

The cows and sheep learned to turn the lights on and off with their snouts. Sheep keep the lights on 82 percent of the time each day. Cows like 10 percent less light.

Don't lace me in. It was a dog's life for army units in the icy regions of Alaska, especially for the dogs. Then the army designed a new boot for its canine soldiers. Now it's a dog's life for everyone except the dogs.

The new boot replaced an earlier canvas-and-leather model, which had to be laced, and often slipped off. Human soldiers suffered from frozen fingers after lacing the boots for a dog team in subzero weather. The men were casualties before the dogs were.

So the Army Research and Development Laboratory at Natick, Massachusetts, came up with a nylon-and-deerskin model, a smaller boot that is fastened around the dog's ankle with a Velcro strip. The boots come in two sizes, regular and large.

The new footwear was tried out by the U.S. Forestry Service at Mt. McKinley, Alaska, in 1978. The test was a success, and the boots became standard issue.

Hire a hen. Karisa Rothey, 6, of Sandy, Utah, took a page from her state's history and went into business renting chickens.

Back in 1847, before the days of insecticides, sea gulls had helped save Utah settlers from swarms of grasshoppers that were eating crops.

In 1982, Karisa found that birds were still an answer to the insect plague. Hungry bugs were stripping gardens and fruit trees in her hometown. Local officials asked the governor to provide state aid and even call out the Utah National Guard. Karisa had a cheaper method of dealing with the problem.

"All people need are some chickens," Karisa said. "They love to eat bugs. The grasshoppers used to eat all the plants in our garden. We had to plant the corn twice. But the chickens just gobbled up the grasshoppers."

Karisa educated her neighbors and rented them Leghorn chickens by the week. As in days long gone, the birds did the job.

Eternally yours. Bill Shippee, Kansas publisher of the Shawnee *Journal–Herald,* believed dead pets deserve more than a shoebox and a grave in the backyard. In 1983, he began accepting paid notices for them. "It helps people who have lost a pet bid their final farewell."

Shippee ran the animal obituaries next to those of human beings. One dog's obituary read:

Misty, dog hit by car. Favorite trick: Sticking out her paw when someone said, "Give me five, Misty."

Poached salmon. Researchers in Seattle put radio transmitters on salmon to study their movements. In 1978, the researchers were shocked to discover that a couple of salmon were sending signals from dry land.

It turned out that a hungry bear had scooped up two

of the fish and carried them into the woods for dinner. Apparently, Mr. Bear didn't fancy transmitters for dessert.

IV.

Critters and Crimes

Displeased as punch. In Oakland, California, in 1948, a man who was caught jaywalking by a mounted policeman expressed himself bluntly. He upped and socked the policeman's horse.

The horse shook off the blow without any ill effects. The man wasn't so lucky.

He was charged with jaywalking, failure to obey a police officer, and with assault and battery on a police officer because if the punch had dropped the horse, the officer would have been injured.

His master's voice. In 1931, Reese Dupré accused a junkyard dealer of stealing four of his chickens. Police rounded up the chickens and brought them to court in Neptune, New Jersey.

To prove he was the true owner, Dupré, a concert

singer, began to croon "Old Black Joe" to the four birds. Pretty soon a rooster joined the chorus.

That was good enough for the judge.

"When a rooster croons a duet with a man claiming ownership, it's time the fowl be given him," the judge ruled.

Biting the hand that sped him. A valuable white-faced macaw named Pedro attacked and injured the thief who stole it from its cage in 1967.

The bird bit Armando Silva on the hand, causing him to crash his motorcycle as he sped from the bird farm, Jungla de Suarez, in Panama. Police found Pedro perched on a bush a few feet from Silva. The luckless thief lay pinned under his motorcycle, his ankle broken.

"A macaw," said a spokeswoman for the bird farm, "is like any other animal—it gets excited and might bite when somebody grabs it. And when it grabs you, that means trouble. A macaw can bite a broomstick in half."

Pedro was not hurt in the crash. It welcomed the police with a cheery "Hello."

Silva needed treatment for a bird bite between his left index finger and thumb as well as for his broken ankle.

Safety deposit. Raymond Graham Jones, owner of the Southhams Zoo in England, took a tiger along when he brought his money to the bank in 1979.

With Rita, a 3-year-old tiger, in tow to guard against muggers, Jones made his deposit safely. The bank had been cleared ahead of time.

"I couldn't risk losing customers," said Raymond Beddoes, the bank manager, "but I asked him not to bring the tiger with him again."

The place was bugged. A pair of burglars were frightened out of a Cleveland, Ohio, apartment in 1982. They knocked over the cage of a deadly pet tarantula named Charlotte, allowing her to escape.

"When they saw Charlotte come out, they split," Patrolman Walter L. Meyke said.

Police caught up with the two suspects. Charlotte remained at large.

Once is not enough. Mildred Thomas identified the thief who stole her wallet—twice. The police caught the suspect, but there wasn't anything they could do.

"We can't arrest a dog," a police sergeant said. "A dog can run up and take anything he wants."

In 1981, Thomas was sitting outside her apartment building in Kansas City, Missouri. She had a bag containing groceries and her wallet on a bench beside her. An Afghan hound walked up, grabbed the bag, and ran off.

Within minutes a neighborhood boy had recovered the bag, but the dogged dog came back. Nosing into the bag, it bypassed a packet of lunch meat, snatched the wallet, and bounded off again.

The dog was traced to its owner's home a short distance away. The owner couldn't believe the theft. The best police could do was fill out a report. The wallet was never found, and there was no proof that the dog was a trained thief.

The trouble with stealing a parrot. Inspector Enio Araujo, a 22-year police veteran in the town of Canoas, Brazil, knew something was amiss in 1982 when he overheard Blondy, a parrot, screaming, "Big Baby!"

Big Baby happened to be the nickname of Jorge Luis Santos, 18, a youth with a record of bird stealing.

Blondy's new owner swore he had received the bird as a gift from a friend. Later, he admitted buying the parrot.

The inspector had a hunch: The person who sold the parrot was none other than Big Baby, the bird thief. Blondy was taken into custody. Big Baby was brought to headquarters, along with his sidekick, a brother.

Big Baby stayed calm. He insisted he'd never before laid eyes on Blondy. So the inspector prodded the parrot. Blondy started up with a loud "Big Baby!" and repeated the name again and again.

"Don't believe him, inspector," Big Baby cried. "He's a liar. You know what parrots are like!"

It was a standoff—Big Baby's word against Blondy's. The inspector had a good idea who really owned the parrot. He summoned her. Blondy hopped onto her shoulder and rubbed her face. That clinched the case.

Big Baby's brother broke down and confessed to the theft. "The bird gave us away!" he wailed.

Vive la difference. Two English tourists went to prison because they didn't know the difference between dogs and drugs.

Reilly Dibely and Sonia Dempsey, both 26, were arrested on suspicion of possessing illegal drugs in 1982. French police found a bag of white powder in their camper near Ramatuelle on the Côte d'Azur.

A policeman held up the bag and, using the French word for drugs, inquired, *"Drogues?"*

"Oh, yes, dogs," Dibely laughingly agreed.

Drogues and dogs sounded a little alike. The French policeman didn't understand English any better than the English couple understood French. He promptly tossed them into *le clink* for three days.

The bewildered couple thought they had agreed to the truth. The powder was a repellent used to discourage dogs from relieving themselves on their camper.

Inside job. Kevin and Ramona Murray called the police in Northfield, Michigan, in 1981. Ramona's diamond ring had been stolen.

While police checked for signs of forced entry, the Murrays did some sleuthing themselves. They got a metal detector and made a sweep of their home.

The detector was as silent as a clam till it was placed near their cat, Smokey. Then it beeped wildly.

Smokey was whisked to the veterinarian and X-rayed. The couple's suspicions were confirmed. Smokey had swallowed the ring.

Doberman pinched. John Scaward's used car lot in Tampa, Florida, was robbed six times in two months. So he paid $350 for Max, a nine-month-old Doberman pinscher trained to bark, snarl, and snap at strangers.

Max seemed the ideal choice as a watchdog—until one night in 1983.

Thieves struck again. They ignored the used cars. They knew what they wanted, what was of value. They stole Max. They led him out (as his pawprints showed), along with his chain, his $38 collar, his food dish, and a 25-pound sack of dog food.

"I don't see how they stole the dog," said a puzzled Scaward. "I just got him to where I could control him."

It's an ill wind. A federal jury in Tyler, Texas, awarded a couple $195,000 damages in 1981 because a chicken hatchery across the road gave their home a bad odor.

Snake in bad company. A store manager in Hempstead, New York, was robbed at snakepoint in 1981.

Anthony Ditaranto asked two men and a woman to leave his Radio Shack store so that he could close for the night. One of the men pulled back his Windbreaker to reveal a black-and-orange snake coiled around his waist.

The man invited Ditaranto to touch the snake and then told him it was poisonous.

"I wasn't going to argue," Ditaranto said. "I was really scared it would bite me."

As Ditaranto stepped back, the snake-hipped thief cleaned out the cash register, and disappeared into the night with his friends, both human and reptilian.

How tweet it isn't. Jane Messina of Braintree, Massachusetts, went to court in 1980. After two years, her pet cockatoo, Sheba, hadn't uttered a word, and cockatoos are supposed to talk like crazy. Messina blamed the pet shop that sold her the bird.

She sued for damages and lost.

"There are some birds that won't talk no matter how much time you spend with them," testified Dr. Margaret Petrak, a Boston veterinarian.

The judge agreed. Birds, he remarked, are like humans. "Some are smarter than others."

Sheba, the strong, dumb type, had no comment.

He flew thataway. A crow in British Columbia turned to a life of crime.

Travelers passing through Prince George Airport in 1979 were warned to keep an eagle eye on their belongings. The crow stole parking tickets from cars and small items left outside the airport building.

After travelers were alerted, the robber bird flew away in search of easier pickings.

Polly want a smacker? A parrot landed behind bars in 1982 after bad-mouthing a police officer.

The bird was sent to the animal shelter while his owner was held briefly on a drunk-driving charge.

Patrolman Dave Boyce of Memphis, Tennessee, had flagged down the car driven by the bird's owner. Approaching the vehicle, Boyce heard cursing coming from the front seat. He warned the driver to mind his language. The driver shrugged innocently and pointed to a green parrot perched on the steering wheel.

"As soon as I read them their rights, the bird shut up," said Boyce.

Ugly is as ugly does. Carolos Salvador da Silva, 22, known in his neighborhood as Dodo, needed some extra money to celebrate Rio de Janeiro's carnival in 1982. Shortly before dawn, he broke into the home of Adelino Braga.

Dodo found an electric fan and an iron and put them into a sack. He searched on, looking for cash and jewels, and making too much noise. His bumbling wakened Braga and his wife, who screamed, "There's a thief in the house!"

Dodo dashed outside and was caught in the lights switched on by startled neighbors. Panicking, he sought a hiding place in the Bragas' large backyard.

When the police arrived, they could not find the thief. Dodo had jumped into an old bathtub and was crouching down next to what he thought was a log.

The log was a sleeping, 12-year-old alligator named Ugly.

With the daylight, Ugly the alligator stirred. His eyes fell on what might be a tasty breakfast—Dodo. At the same time Dodo saw the "log" bare its teeth.

First Dodo's hair stood up, and then he did. He leaped from the bathtub yelling, "Let me out of here!"

The police obliged.

Run for it. The great pet shop escape attempt of 1981 nearly succeeded.

The daring midnight breakout was foiled by a policeman, Steve Vorley. He shone his flashlight into the window of the Animal Magic Pet Shop in London, England, and stared in disbelief. A monkey was swinging around the shop, unlatching cages.

Chimp, a tiny 2-year-old South American Capuchin monkey, had bitten through the wire of his cage. Wriggling free, he released his fellow prisoners—24 birds, 20 mice, and 12 lizards.

Officer Vorley called for backup. By the time nine policemen arrived, the shop was in ruins. Birds were flying around in circles, mice and lizards were running hither and yon. Dog biscuits, bird seed, and other pet food lay strewn over the floor. Fish tanks were shattered.

The police used their helmets to trap the animals. They cast fishing nets to catch the birds. When the other escapees were captured, Chimp, the ringleader, gave up quietly.

Sweet tooth. Someone or something set off the burglar

alarm three times in six weeks in Bruce Olson's liquor store in Corona Del Mar, California, in 1980. Strangely, all that was stolen was candy—more than 900 bars of Pay Days, Milky Ways, and Three Musketeers.

Olson finally cornered the thief—a squirrel. It was building a nest under some shelves and hoarding the goodies.

Aside from the ruined candy bars, the squirrel cost Olson $75 in fines from the police department because of the false alarms. They sounded when the squirrel chewed on the wires.

Olson wasn't vengeful. He set the tiny thief loose in a quiet, pleasant field—far from his store.

Loyalty is a sometime thing. A Texas poacher was betrayed by his own dog.

The Texas Parks and Wildlife Department investigated a routine report in 1980: A man had shot a deer out of season and had taken it home. Game Warden Jesse May and three other wardens obtained a search warrant. They drove to the suspect's house but saw no signs of a deer.

As they were leaving, the man's bird dog trotted up to their car. In its jaws was the leg bone of a deer.

May took the bone, and the dog spun and trotted toward the barn—with the wardens following. A careful inspection behind the barn turned up parts of two deer, plus several raw pelts.

The dog's owner blew his top.

"That blankety-blank dog never retrieved anything for *me*!" he said.

110

Bird droppings. A Hong Kong jeweler used pigeons to obtain money from the Shell Oil Company. In 1982, Chong Shing-keung tried to collect $75,000 in bags strapped to the backs of homing pigeons as payment for not bombing the company's property.

Police in helicopters followed the money. But the

downdraft from the rotor blades drove the pigeons off course and scattered them. Shing-keung was later captured in a telephone booth while calling the oil company with another demand. He was sentenced to 15 years in prison.

How big is that doggie near the window? A teenager had chopped a hole in the wall of a store in 1980. Once inside, he tripped an alarm. Police surrounded the building in Phoenix, Arizona, but the youth refused to come out.

Officer Steve Gregory shouted that if he didn't surrender, a vicious police dog would be sent in. When the teenager wouldn't budge, Officer Al Femina growled and barked with the savagery of a German shepherd.

The youth hollered, "Don't let the dog loose! I'm coming out!"

Stepping outside, he looked uneasily around for the dog and saw only grinning policemen.

The high cost of dropping in. Bats and pigeons that dwelt in the rafters of the century-old jail in Hamilton County, Ohio, left a $400,000 mess that was too costly to clean up. The county had set aside only $30,000 for the job.

"The whole building isn't worth $400,000," said County Administrator Michael Maloney in 1983.

A new jail was built.

Quacking down on crime. The epidemic of rabies

that all but killed off Hong Kong's dog population led to the discovery of a better burglar alarm—the duck.

Nearly 42,000 dogs died or had to be destroyed during a three-month period in 1980. Villagers in Hong Kong's New Territories along the Chinese frontier were afraid to leave their homes unguarded in the face of rising crime. So they began boosting duck production.

The villagers had discovered that a quack—or, in Chinese, a *yawk*—served better than a bark when it comes to protecting property.

"Dogs will only bark at passing strangers, not at villagers," said Won Pak, 67, a duck farmer. As an example, he told of his 16-year-old cousin, a frequent visitor, who tried to sneak into his house to steal his money. "He might have succeeded," Pak said, "if I had not been awakened by the ducks."

Fastest gun with a pest. Michael F. Rasmussen, Jr., of Atlanta admitted to police in 1964 that he'd shot out his neighbor's electric bug-killer with a .22 rifle. Rasmussen explained that the device triggered his sensitive burglar alarm every time it zapped a bug.

Cops and clobbers. For two summers a mockingbird with a grudge attacked police officers in Norfolk, Virginia.

"We think he got a ticket somewhere in the past," Sergeant R. F. Miller said.

114

The feathered fury appeared in 1981, and dwelt in a row of trees lining a parking lot used by police and other city employees. He swooped down on anyone but mainly on police, clobbering their heads and arms with his beak.

"This bird was trained by the RAF," Officer J. C. Thomas said. "He gets you quiet. It's like the death stalk."

Officer Mike Kinney was attacked three times in one day. "You hear that flapping behind you about the time he hits you," Kinney said. "It's got me gun-shy."

Early attempts to arrest the bird failed. A judge claimed the police didn't have enough evidence. Then, after a few months of looking over their shoulders, the officers mellowed. They developed a certain fondness for the fowl fiend. He became a mascot.

"He's like our own Loch Ness monster," Officer Thomas said. "You think we want to do away with our landmark?"

Eventually, it was a point of honor to be clobbered. A policeman would come in and announce, "Hey, I just got strafed by the bird."

Such favorable reactions must have burned up the mockingbird. He refused to return for a third summer of aerial assaults.

This can't be love. A prizewinning show horse needed 100 stitches after being attacked in 1937 by a man wielding an ax and a pitchfork in Jersey City. The man told police the horse reminded him of his wife.

Left-all-alone-again blues. Australian customs officers frisked a nervy traveler from Bali in 1979. They found five pythons he was trying to smuggle into the country in pouches strapped to his legs and in his underpants.

They only ate lefties. From 1934 until 1962, Alcatraz was a prison to which only dangerous troublemakers from other prisons were sent. Built upon 12 acres of solid rock and surrounded entirely by water, it was considered "escape-proof." To gain their freedom, inmates had to break out of the walls and then swim across more than a mile of water to the San Francisco mainland.

An added obstacle was the natural fear of sharks—a horror the guards played upon. They told the prisoners (not a real bright bunch) that Alcatraz was surrounded by circling great white sharks. According to the guards, each man-eater had its right fin removed by surgery so that it could swim only in circles around the island.

ABOUT THE AUTHOR

DONALD J. SOBOL is the author of the highly acclaimed Encyclopedia Brown books. His awards for these books include the Pacific Northwest Reader's Choice Award for *Encyclopedia Brown Keeps the Peace* and a special Edgar from the Mystery Writers of America for his contribution to mystery writing in the United States.

Donald Sobol is married and has three children. A native of New York, he now lives in Florida.

ABOUT THE ILLUSTRATOR

TED ENIK is a playwright, set designer, magazine artist, and cartoonist as well as a children's book illustrator. He is the illustrator of *Bob Fulton's Terrific Time Machine* by Jerome Beatty, Jr.; the Sherluck Bones Mystery-Detective books by Jim and Mary Razzi; and several books in Bantam's Choose Your Own Adventure series, including *The Curse of Batterslea Hall*, *The Creature from Miller's Pond*, and *Summer Camp*. Mr. Enik lives in New York City.